I Must Go to the Well

I Must Go

To Keith with gratitude—
for sharing with me via e-mail
his much more active life
Greatly expanding my limited
horizons—
with love, Mary

to the Well

Word pictures from a woman's soul

by Mary V. Borhek

Mary V. Borhek

NELSON BORHEK PRESS
Minneapolis, Minnesota

ISBN: 978-0-9843002-1-1
Library of Congress Control Number: 2011901413

Front cover: Illustration based on a photograph, "Well in Cameroun," ©Lutheran World Federation/J. Latva-Hakuni. Used with permission.

Back cover: Author photo by Susan M. Dreydoppel.

Nelson Borhek Press
Minneapolis, Minnesota
www.nelsonborhek.com

Printed in the United States of America

To my three (wonderful) children
Sue, Steve, Betsy

Also by Mary Borhek:

My Son Eric

Coming Out to Parents

Contents

I Must Go
to the Well

Introduction

Cleaning out old files usually is about as much fun as going to the dentist. However . . . .

Recently, my son Steve ("Eric" of *My Son Eric*) was helping me go through some old files when I came upon one labeled "My Poems." Between 1975 and 1990 I had written quite a number of poems which I had put into a folder and then totally forgotten.

During those years, I was occupied with a great many other things. In 1971, my husband had gotten a divorce, leaving me utterly devastated. It took a number of years before I could pull myself together and find a new direction to my life. Ironically, it was the discovery in 1975 that Steve was gay that finally led to the necessary changes in my outlook. I tried to find a counselor for Steve—hoping he could be changed from gay to straight—except I was the one who ended up going for counseling. I, not Steve, was the one who changed. I have told that story in my book, *My Son Eric*.

For the first time in my life I began to find out who I was, aside from fulfilling a number of roles—daughter, sister, minister's wife, mother. Through counseling I began to separate my real self from the roles I had played. I had always had a prose voice, but now I found I also had a poetic one.

Subsequently I went on to write another book, *Coming Out to Parents*, and was invited to speak and hold workshops in many different locations throughout the country. In addition, I participated in radio and TV programs having to do with homosexuality.

Years passed and I began to realize that I needed to make some decisions about my future. I sold my house in Minnesota and moved back to Bethlehem, Pennsylvania, which I had left 41 years earlier. I spent seven years in Bethlehem before moving to a lifecare retirement center in Bucks County, Pennsylvania. Poetry was nowhere in my thinking during these transition years.

But I apparently had left my bucket near the well, and now, with the inspiration of my earlier poems, I was moved to write a few more. Most fortuitously, in addition to his day job, Steve has established Nelson Borhek Press. How lucky can a mother be!

So the poems that spent years in a folder are now seeing the light of day. Through them I can share with you a bit of my heart and soul. I'm so glad we found these files, so glad I found my bucket, so glad I found the well.

Finding the Path

I Must Go to the Well

I must go to the well again
    and draw water.
The well is very deep
    and I am tired.
I do not know if the rope I have
    is long enough
    and I have lost my bucket.

Perhaps there is a bucket there
    waiting,
and I can throw it in
    and draw it up,
full of life-giving water
    to quench my thirst.

I will go to the well and look.
I think I left my bucket there.

First Seeing

My seeing began
the day my husband
asked for a divorce.

I went out
and drove through the countryside,
and it was as if
I had never seen the world before—
each scene stood out sharply etched:
azure sky
fierce golden sun
trees of such green it pierced my heart
wheat bending like waves coming to shore
    —but never breaking—

and tears rained down my face
for the beauty of the world amid the ruin
    of my life,
as if some giant hand had cracked and split
the tight shell in which I had been encased.

Faith

Hot tears in the night.
I have reached the end of known territory.
Beyond?
How did Columbus feel
setting out
when everyone was sure that out beyond
there was nothing
and when he reached that edge
he would fall off
and disappear?
He had courage
or faith.
I have gone to the limits of myself.
Beyond there is only darkness.
I cannot see.
Now is the time to stand
And make a ringing declaration of my faith.
But my voice fails; my legs are weak.
And I can only say,
"God, I've gone as far as I can go.
I'm alone. I'm frightened.
Take my hand
    and then I'll know
that this is not the end
that dawn always comes
    somehow
    some way . . ."

O God I Am Angry With You

O God
I am angry with you
    and because of this
        I am afraid.
One does not lightly hurl defiance
    at the universe's Lord.

I am afraid—
    afraid to be close.
Proximity to me has meant
        pain.
Those closest to me
    have wounded me
    or I have wounded them.

O God,
will I have the courage
    to try
    again?

One Foot Forward

O God, when the way ahead is obscured by thick fog,
when all around there is an enshrouding nothingness;
when the only thing I can see is just enough path ahead
so that I can place one foot forward —

please, God, empower my foot.

House Call

God, I cannot go to church today.
I cannot give anything of myself away
even to you.

What I need, God, is a house call.
If you are willing to come and give whatever I ask
you may come. But don't ask me for anything
because I don't have it.

Don't give me what I don't want, either.
I don't need beauty or music or fair words
or hope or faith or even love right now.

All I need is healing for the deep ugly wounds
far down inside me where nobody sees them.
Don't talk to me about the cross and death and
resurrection.
I don't want to hear any of that now.
Don't talk.
Just put your hand deep inside me and heal my wounds.

(I am indebted to Peter McWilliams, one of the three authors of the
book, *How to Survive the Loss of a Love*, for the idea of God making a
house call on Sunday.)

The Key

I have spent the morning
in solitude,
wrapped in a blanket,
sitting warm in bed
visiting with a Friend.

He comes to me
anytime He chooses
but I find that
solitude helps.

Often it is because of those times of solitude
that I hear Him
at busier times.

This morning,
wrapped in a blanket
because of this new phenomenon we call
the "energy crisis"
I was letting my spirit wander
with His Spirit

and suddenly
I was overwhelmed by a glimpse
deep, deep into the secrets
of the universe

of the Eternal
of the Never-ending God

and I cried
noiselessly
within myself,
"O yes! That's it!
It's all so plain
and simple.
Somehow I did not really understand
before."

The problem of pain,
of suffering,
of death,

of war,
disease,
poverty —

why did I not see?
Why did I not
understand?

Even this energy crisis
and all the ecological problems
of our little planet
and all the pain in my life
(there has been plenty of that) —
why did I not see?

None of these things
is an end
of anything.

There is no end
as there was no beginning.
The world is not flat
but round
and eternally there are
circles
cycles
seasons
tides which
ebb and flow

and still we have not understood
the awesome Paradox of God
which He has told us
over and over
in a thousand ways.

A thousand?
No, a million
billion
trillion
zillion ways.

What is this
stupendous secret?
What is this
Paradox of God?

It drenches me.
My heart pounds.
I can hardly breathe.

During the night I asked Him

for a word.
"You used to speak to me," I said.
"Maybe I haven't asked lately,
haven't expected;
but I ask You now."

He gave me not one word
but four
and suddenly
the riddles of the Universe
are plain.

Bind them as a sign upon your hand;
wear them as frontlets to your eyes;
write them on the doorposts of your house.
But most of all
know them deep within your heart—
the key on which the Universe is founded—
"Out of death—life!"

Moses

Instinctively I know
it is not yet the time
when soul can soar
and fetters will fall free.

Still must I walk
this earthbound path,
bruising my foot
on rocky soil,
struggling and climbing,
breathless and lathered,
until I reach a ridge.

Then I can pause
and breathe
and see
stretching before me in the distance
the Promised Land.

The Alchemists' Stone

Philosophers and alchemists of
    the Middle Ages
searched
for the alchemists' stone
which would change
worthless metals to
gold.

They searched
in the wrong place.

God has the true alchemists' stone,
    nine simple words
        that,
    given time,
can change the direst defeat
    to victory:

    "Nothing
     that is given to Me
     is ever wasted."

I Sit at the Edge of the Pool

I sit at the edge of the pool,
the water covering my feet.
I sit among the reeds and grasses.
The water is deep, very deep.
There is no limit to the depth.
Only my feet are in the water.
Sometimes with my hands
I reach into the water,
draw handfuls
and pour it over myself,
over my body.

Some day perhaps I shall swim in this pool
unafraid.

David Said It Best

David said it best:
"Yea, though I walk through the valley
    of the shadow of death
I will fear no evil, for
Thou
art with me."

And who was it said,
"The thing which I greatly feared
has come upon me?"*

I am walking
    through deserts
Climbing mountains
Facing dragons
    and dinosaurs
Evil ogres
    prehistoric men
Lions
    banshees
        witches

That which I feared
so greatly that I thrust it from me —
I am looking at it,
I am facing it.

I am walking through
the valley of the shadow
of death

only because
You
are with me.

And because
You
have shown me
that
when I have come through
    the valley
there is life
on the other side.

Who is Me?

I wonder,
Who is me?

Maybe
If I sit very quietly,
Me will come
And show I
Who.

No Crime

Pound pillows
Punch the air
Slam doors
Kick emptiness.
It is no crime
To feel.

I think God
Wants real feeling
Much more than
Empty piousness

Earthquake

Earthquake!
Everything is going,
 slipping,
  sliding,
   crashing,
 shifting,
  rocking,
   reassembling,
 moving again into new shapes.
I am in a hall of mirrors.
What I thought was solid
 was only a reflection,
  a shifting of light
  against another shaft of light
There was a wall there
 but now there isn't.
The wall didn't move. It dissolved.
It is no more.
In its place is space — space without boundaries.
The old boundaries rasped and rubbed

they limited view
    and movement
but they were at least safe —
    you knew where you were.
You might not like it, and you might
chafe
    but at least there were limits —
there are no limits now —
the walls are in a crazy jumble,
at all angles,
    slipping and sliding —
maybe the floor is a wall
or part of a ceiling —
I don't know if I am standing on the floor
    or the ceiling
        or maybe the window —

I don't know what way is up because I am in the middle of an earthquake and at the moment everything is

TOPSY TURVY
where did those two words
    come from?
who invented them?
I am trying to find footprints in
a swamp

The Rainmaker

It is one of those stories with which
the mind plays endlessly, fascinated:
the Rainmaker in his hut, going
about his daily business,
eating, sleeping, cooking, washing,
just being —

but being so simply and totally that he becomes
one with the universe, living so deep within
himself that he is in touch with the core
of the earth, the depths of the ocean,
the reach of the stars, and has charted
his unknowable Self. And if you asked him,
"What is love?" he would look at you and smile
and say, "Love is being." Yet I know that for me

to be is not always love. And I know
that for me to go about my daily business
would not bring the rain desperately needed,
or stop the deluging torrents, or turn the
raging winds into playful breezes.

What is the oneness with creation that
you have attained, Rainmaker? How
can I attain it? We have plumbed
the universe with our polished glasses and our
ships that defy space, with our magical
mechanical minds that answer us in a
split second with information it would
take us years to figure. We could destroy
our world tomorrow if that was what we
wanted to do. We have the means locked
into tubes and cans and boxes, death
waiting to happen.

Why is it so difficult to learn how to love?

I Have Been Striving

I have been striving
       hustling
          bustling
    organizing
    doing
         accomplishing
    fitting   a schedule
      quite exactly.

I must sit down now,
    quietly,
beside the pool,
among the reeds and rushes,

    and

    just

    be.

Ezekiel 37:1-14 Updated

I have to go down deeper into myself,
into the clay and stone and granite

until I reach the bottom chamber,
the grey, dim, shadowy, dusty
place of nothingness

and there I will find old statues,
broken remnants, bones, shards, fragments,

out of which I will fashion
a new, strong, living, beautiful
Self

a gift
from Goddess
to goddess.

God Is Not Dead

The pattern is used
not once but many times

over
and over and
over
creatively
not monotonously.

The atom
foreshadows the universe
and the universe
the atom.

The inner war
becomes the outer.

God is within
but Other
and beyond.

The mind reflects the body
and the body
the mind

and the most real thing in all
the world
may be our dreams.

New Vistas

We lived in a small room without windows
    God and I, quite happily for awhile.
One day, I began fussing with the lock
    on the door.
At last I opened the door
    and went through it.
I had to.
There was no other way.
I had thought it was dark out there.
I had thought maybe I was leaving God
    back there in that room.
What a surprise to find that
    all the while
He had been preparing a limitless garden
    for me.
It stretches as far as my eye can see
    and beyond.
All the time, He had been out there
    waiting for me.

Nature in my life

Daffodil

Daffodil, I love you —
saffron trumpet,
aureate star,
chrysoprase leaves
piercing dull clods,
reaching for heaven —
answering the glory of the sun
with your own shining passion.

I Must Sit Quietly

I must sit down
        quietly
beside the pool
among the reeds and grasses.
I must watch the curved fronds
        of the weeping willows,
fluid motion in the breeze.

I must wait
        quietly
for a butterfly
to come silently,
        delicately,
a jewel floating gently
        on the air.

I must wait
        patiently
for a bird to come,
a tiny spark of life
        within bright plumage.

I Am a Tree

I am a tree.
I live deep underneath the earth
and lift towards heaven.

In spring
I feel the gentle rain
Slanting through my bare boughs
and against my parched trunk.
And from deep, deep in the earth
I feel answering moisture
rise within me
little by little
filling every cell
from the deep roots
to the topmost twig.

I feel the warmth of the sun
penetrating
penetrating
till the joy of it
goes from the topmost twig

down to the deep roots
and I know that
again
I am alive.

In summer
I feel the heat,
the breezes,
the crashing tumultuous winds,
the days when all is stifling
and my leaves hang limp.
I am growing,
growing,
nourished by the fullness I draw from the sun,
by the strength I draw through my infinite network of
roots
from the soil.
I am full,
I am strong
in summer.

All summer
I am gathering,
gathering,
storing life, and life, and more life
until finally
life bursts from me
in ecstasy of gold, russet, scarlet, orange, copper, wine—
my glory more and more glorious
in the sun,
flaming and wheeling
in a leaping, dazzling tumult of color

like continuing fireworks
over
and over
and over
until

Suddenly
I am spent,

dying in autumn madness
of wind
and rain.

And the life giving silver liquid
recedes
deep into the earth
as the cold
creeps
ever closer,
deeper,
until I am surrounded
penetrated
filled
with cold
and death.
I look out
over a white
silver
blue
and shining
world,
beautiful beyond measure,

but cold,
still,
waiting,
waiting,
waiting for the day
when life will rise up
and fill me
fuller
and fuller
and fuller
and I will know again
there is a God.

.

Autumn Morning

I stand on the hill
Overlooking the valley.
The morning haze of autumn hangs soft and blue
Above the gold of treetops.
Most of the leaves are gone now.
At this distance the bare branches
Look like grey mist among the still bright trees.
No longer are the flaming reds
Flinging their banners upward to blue sky.
Now they are russet leaves rustling underfoot.
Dark green of pine,
Blue of mist,
Grey of bare branches,
Still defiant gold of clinging leaves —
And over all the slanting morning sun
Touching into fire a world still beautiful.

Hyacinth Memories

(After a hard Minnesota winter — 1982)

I can smell it now,
the greenhouse,
in the days of my childhood.
Sometime the week before Easter
we would visit the greenhouse
and choose flowers for the graves.

We would enter the greenhouse,
walking on the no-frills cement floor
through a long room filled with seedlings,
roofed and sided with the milky painted glass rectangles
of a working greenhouse.

We would enter the sales area —
no carpeting, just a splintery wood floor,
a long splintery counter
with a roll of florists' green paper
on an iron stand at the end of the counter
and of course the glass-encased cooler.

From there we would be taken
to an octopus arm of the greenhouse
where the hyacinths grew.

I can remember standing in the doorway,
being drenched in that
fresh, damp, green, spicy smell
and seeing the rows and rows of spiked blooms,
cream, pink, blue-violet, white,
as if all the stars of the Milky Way

had sifted to earth and been caught
on a thousand green columns
here in the greenhouse.

We would walk damp earthen paths between
the endless pots of blooms
and I was like a bee
drunk on the sparkling tingling smell
of hyacinths. And my mother said,
"I'll take a pink one for Henry's father,
a cream one for his mother,
a white one for my grandfather,
a blue one for my mother—"
a litany of their dead.
But to me the ritual, the greenhouse, the hyacinths
did not speak of death,
they spoke of life.

To me this was the smell of spring—
wet earth and moss and gently growing things,
a smell of fragrant stars
that lit my heart,
filling me with fresh newness
like some earth rite, ancient and pure,
of wood nymphs and new moons
and spring—
telling me that
winter always vanished in eternal cycle,
bringing life again.

Today I must buy a hyacinth.
I need these hyacinth memories.

Dawn to Sunrise

I waked early,
in time to see the sky turn
from indigo to cobalt to the
mother-of-pearl of dawn —
blush of rose, wash of mermaid green,
pale saffron, gentle azure
all intermingled
in a soft luminescence
lighting the corridor for the gleaming sun
before it burst the shroud of horizons
and rode triumphantly up the steeps of heaven
to begin another day.

Dune

Sand and thin grasses
bending ceaselessly in the wind.
There are stones and shells and sky,
and the waves rising endlessly,
rolling, breaking,
over
    and over
        and over
          and over.
I lie against the sand
warmed and cleansed by the sun,
and a spring opens up
    within me.

Fruition

Out of the dark secret loam of suffering
a white narcissus blooms.

Aquarelle

The sky is blue, serene.
The surface of the lake is still.
The air is calm. No breeze
ruffles the mirrored peace.

Fathoms deep
the lake's real life goes on.
There is a tempest,
dark and fell, violent,
black with pain
that stirs and heaves and thrashes
to and fro.
Far, far beneath
it thunders, rumbles, roils and heaves
while up above

all is calm
bright
beautiful.

Magic

This morning there is ice fog
veiling the world I see
from my bedroom window.

Instead of plain white fields,
blue sky, brisk sunshine,
leafless trees
I am inside an iridescent pearl.
Two frost-flocked saplings
flank our entering drive.
Beyond, a mist, a cloud
luminous and glowing,
rosy with dawn.

Above the edges of this rosy mist,
springing from nowhere,
the disembodied tops of phantom trees,
a filigree of pearl.

So Asgard, Camelot,
and fair Elysium
looked

and common fields and farms and trees
are changed into a magic dream
with Nature's mad enchantment.

Just an Ordinary Friday

Morning.
Just an ordinary Friday.
Nothing special.

Dawn.
Deep tender blue sky
paling to peach-wheat,
then rose
shading to amethyst-grey
just at the horizon.
Black tracery of trees
silhouetted.

Soon the unbelievable
huge burning red-orange
incandescent rim of the sun
will show
above the horizon.

Look quickly.
In minutes he will be
higher, smaller,
fading to gold —
an everyday sun.

Morning.
Just an ordinary Friday.
Nothing special.
Then why
such lavish beauty?

I Thought the Autumn Colors Gone

I thought the autumn colors gone.
The blazing gold and scarlet leaves
Are now a dry and rustling carpet underfoot.
Now come the subtler shades:
The liquid silver of a misty pond
Touched by the rising sun.
Around its rim are grasses, rusty now,
And at one side a tree,
Its yellowed leaves
Lit into gold by slanting beams of light.

I drive—and see a hillside lit
Into a thousand colors.
No more the flat bright green of summer.
Now in the green
Are pink and beige, deep wine and honey gold,
Pale wheat and, in the grass and trees,
A hundred shades of russet.

There is a royal carpet on that autumn hill,
Lit by the shafted glory
Of the newly risen sun.

People, known and unknown

To Dad on Father's Day, June, 1976

Where have you gone?
Once you were,
    and now you are not.
Where did you go?

My head tells me words about
             immortality
but my heart does not hear them.
All I know is you are gone
    and I miss you.

But you have left me a precious
          legacy,
for instance, your love for growing
          things.

I think you did not speak to plants
but they felt your touch,
they knew your care.
They grew
and multiplied and blossomed
          for you.
As life's fevers calmed you became
          a philosopher.

Not that you sat and talked
endlessly.
Your philosophy was lived.
"If I cannot fish
I will paint;
if I can no longer paint
I will write;
as I write I will be a friend."
And you became in time a lover—
not in the sense in which the
young and passionate use the word
but in the ripe and mellow caring,
in the opening of your heart, yourself,
to others.

Age may have withered your body
but your heart, your mind,
expanded, grew, ripened, mellowed
till at last
you were what man was meant to be—
wise, loving, ageless.
And then at the pinnacle
you stepped through the door

and left me memories . . . and money.

I do not despise the money.
I enjoy it.
I have things I never had before
and every one a gift from you.

But if I had to choose I would say,
"The memories are the greater treasure.
I will keep those."

The Writer

"... the writer, a hermit in the
   cave of his mind ..."

I sit far back in my cave
      holding out a paper doll
            on a stick
so that people going by
      will see the paper doll
            and think it is I

while all the time
            safe from disclosure
      I am living deep within
            absorbing   thinking
            learning   amalgamating
            synthesizing   creating

I sit far back in my cave
      holding out a paper doll
            on a stick

Sarah

Small perfect person
with the right number of
    curly pink fingers
and straight pink toes,
what bright land did you come from
    to our earth plane?

Who taught you to search constantly,
    as I hold you standing
        on my lap,
for balance, to move
    constantly,
strengthening muscles?

What thoughts go on behind
    your observant eyes?
Are you remembering where

you came from?
Are you wondering who
    the people are who
    surround you?
Do you know who you are —
    a separate person,
    someone's child — of course —
    but belonging only to yourself?

Do you know that you came
    into the world
        alone
that no matter how many people
    fill your life
    you always live
    in your deepest self
        alone
and no matter who is with you
    at the final freeing
    you will go
        alone?

Only that spark inside you,
    the god, the goddess within,
came with you,
    will stay with you
        will go with you.

You —
    each person —
ultimate mystery.

Separation

somehow there must be
    a separation
you must be you
    and I, I

there can no longer be
invisible threads
    joining
you   to   me

I do not think the threads
    must be cut
certainly not torn
just a gradual attenuation
    until
there
    is

        no

           more

             thread

To J--

If I could do it for you I would.
I have been the path and know
that death must precede
    life.

One must step off the precipice
into nothingness, not knowing
    if
but trusting that hands await
or a cloud
or a bird
or an angel
and you will be borne gently
    into newness.

It is impossible to imagine
this could happen when one stands
at the edge of the precipice
    but it can.

If I could do it for you I would.
I cannot, and that is what
learned theologians mean when they talk
dryly and passionlessly about
    free will.

Inner Voyage

I have a neighbor with tip-tilted nose
and lovely eyes, young, confident, adventurous.
At twenty-five she dashes off
to London and Bahrein as if she were
commuting to Chicago.
She has seen half the world

while I, more than twice as old,
have seen so little — outer world, that is.

We live on either side of our partition,
and I hear her building a wall
in her basement. She is busy here
and yonder over the ocean —
young, confident, active.

I am sitting in bed reading,
writing, making poems, painting, sculpting,
feeling, digging, dying, being born,
growing, stretching, thinking, feeling pain,
examining this strange creation —
    I.

She wonders what I do.
"Don't you want to travel?"
And I don't know how to tell her
that simply sitting in my house I have
    perhaps traveled
twice as far as she.

Epistle to James

Being a reply to James W. Woelfel's
"The Death of God: A Belated Personal Postscript"
published in the 12/29/76 issue of Christian Century

Bruiséd spirit,
ask not that Mystery
should fit
thy geometric box.

Give back the cross.
E'en Christus
broke beneath its weight
and in the end
cried out,
"My God   My God
why
hast thou forsaken
me?"

Face God and speak to him
as man to man.
Shout to him
thine anger.

Become a little child,
thy feet still damp from swimming
in the endless ocean.

Feel his hands
touching thy spirit
in dream
in myth
in symbol.

Withdraw
into thine inner chamber.
Catch spirit in clay.
Paint dream.
Feel music.
Breathe poetry in
and out.

Nourish thine inner goddess
until
she stretches out her hand
and gives thee
life.

Then
thy God
shall live.

Free Will

God,
You and I have been friends
    a long time
if I may presume to use
that terminology.

There's this young man, God,
who tried to self-destruct.
He got his tax refund
    and in twelve hours
        it was all over.

He had
    bought a car
        (old, overpriced, a junk heap)
    gone to see his mother
    gotten drunk
    blacked out
    totaled the car
    and almost totaled himself.

God,   the pain is almost too much for me
        to bear.
How do I reach into a situation like this?

He is a child of yours, God.
What are you doing for him?

Time passed
    and the storm of emotion within me
        subsided
until at last I was ready to approach God
in His dwelling of infinite
    Mystery

And then
I heard His answer:
    "I am waiting."

"Waiting?" I breathed, very quiet
    and respectful.
Somehow shouting didn't fit.
"Waiting for what, God?"

And again
    that totally distilled Activity
    crystallized into quietness—
        an icicle in a frozen world
        refracting the cosmic brightness
    of the sun—

His words, pulsing endlessly
    in my heart:
"For him.
I am waiting
    for him."

To Meg

It isn't what you
ought
    or
should

It isn't what
    another
thinks you
ought
    or
should

no matter
how much you
    love
        them.

It's what
you
         think
     feel
   decide
do.

Right?
    or
Wrong?

There is no right or wrong
    to
being.

Many Kinds of Love

How many kinds of love
    are there, I wonder.
I have put my hand
    into a green sunlit meadow
spring carpeted,
    with strange and beautiful flowers
and plucked a fragile blossom.

I don't need
        or want
you all the time.
God forbid.
You are so active—big, young,
    so brimming with life.
I need now to withdraw
    contemplate
    read
    paint
    think
    distill
    create.

But I need
    some corner of your heart,
        a little space that has my name

over the door.
   Some place that is saved
      for me alone.

I need to know that we
      can go our separate ways
but that when one
      or the other
calls
we shall be ready with response.

You first demanded this of me,
         I think,
      and I responded.
And now I have demanded, too.
I have tested that love to see
      if you meant it
      when   you said,
               though not in words,
"I love you.
I am available to you
      when you
      need me."

I wonder if you would know
      what I was talking about
if I said these things to you.
      I think not.

I am afraid that
      to put the words between us
      might destroy the gossamer
strands that bind us.

Miscellany

A poem comes

A poem comes
	fragile as a dream
but I am driving

I cannot write it down

I try to remember

	but

it tiptoes away

Dreamworld

You were there.

Who are you?

I was crossing the bridge
    high above frozen tundra
when suddenly the wooden planks
    sloped steeply down.

I was moving too fast —
    I would have fallen —
but you were there
    holding up your hand to me
    at exactly the moment I needed you.

In a smooth, synchronous motion
    I stretched out my hand
        and took yours.
I came down the steep incline
    safely.

I did not see your face
    but I know
you were young, buoyant, joyous —
    a woman —
from the grace with which
    you reached —
    at the right moment —

from the clasp of your hand
    as in perfect rhythm
I took your hand
    and alighted safely.

Meeting

We had a meeting, you and I,
A fleeting moment treasure,
A glance beneath our usual masks
Impossible to measure.

We passed each day upon the stairs,
We ate at the same table;
But not until the very end
Did love enable.

Southdale Library

I could go to the small local library
and reserve the same books.

Somehow my spirit needs
the open airy spaces
of the big suburban building,
the rank on rank of books
set back, not crowding;
the many reading centers,
the people, borrowers and lenders,
all focused on one thing—
books.

I shall never read every book
on those shelves,
nor even one one-hundredth of them.
I do not use the reading spaces;
I would rather read at home.
I do not speak to all the people,
borrowers and lenders,
beyond the barest need:
"I would like to reserve this book."

And yet,
like a mountain which I never climb
higher than the merest foothill,
it is there
and nourishes my spirit.

Sea-nymph

Undine
naiad
mermaid
sprite —
the words roll off my tongue
    like water rippling gently over stones,
    a stream
    flowing through a forest glen.

Nixie
nereid
sea-nymph
sprite —
there is a dim green pool

where lotuses and water lilies
　　bloom.
Far in the cool green depths
　　these water spirits swim
　　flashing with green and silver grace.

Sometimes I lay aside my air-breathing lungs
　　and plunge deep into the
　　　　cool
　　　　　　green
　　　　　　　　depths
　　and swim,
　　　　and arc
　　　　　　and curve effortlessly
　　borne always by the water
　　　　and the fluid greenness
　　and for a little while
　　I am
　　　　undine
　　　　naiad
　　　　mermaid
　　　　nixie
　　　　nereid
　　　　sea-nymph
　　　　sprite.

The Rose

He took me for a walk
    in the garden.
I had supposed it was full of
    briars, thistles, weeds,
hard, thorny growths,
    unlovely and wounding.

He paused and said, "See, a rose."
I looked.
"But it is black," I said, "and dead."
He only stooped and lifted up its head.
And then I saw a red so deep
it looked like black at first
but as I gazed I saw
within the depth of black a crimson
vivid as blood,
rich and glorious
    beyond measure.

Vision

"God, show me Yourself."   I cried.
    "Give me a vision
     that I may see You
     in Your fullness
     and beauty."

    I lived.
    I walked.

But no vision was vouchsafed

    until I reached
    at last
    a stable

There a newborn lay.

    I knelt and gazed.

    Beyond the infant face
    distant I saw

        tree
        blood
        flame
        water, living,
        light
        vine
        bread
        wine

        Trinity

        Life.

Late Poems

The Gift

A poem is a most delicate creation.
You feel the softest, most fleeting tap on your shoulder
    as it flies by.
You reach out to grasp it — here — no, here — no, there —
    it eludes you.
You can almost see it — not quite —
You seem to hear faint words — almost.

And then — suddenly — unexpectedly —
    it is there in your hand —
an undeserved gift to you from the universe.

The Hour Before Sunset

I went out into the gentle air.
The sky was a tender blue,
brushed here and there
with thin white clouds.
I saw her white face
against the blue,
rounded, nearing full.
I always feel better
when I see the moon.

Humiliation

I went to the florist's shop
to buy some flowers for a friend.
A clerk came to wait on me.
The door opened
and suddenly I was talking to empty air.

A woman had come in
with a pot-bellied pig on a leash.
The staff all gathered round.
Some brought old flowers for the pig to eat.

I left without buying any flowers.

I Never Got to London

I never got to London,
I never got to Paris.
The money I would have spent on travel
went to my inner journey
and I have found as I have gotten older
the inner journey was beyond price.

Pansies

"Faces or no faces?" the gardener asked me.
"Oh—faces!" I said.
What is a pansy without a face!

Age

Age is just a number, they say.
But when the barometer is falling
and the humidity is high,
when every joint and muscle in your body hurts,
you know — they lie!

The Witch Tree

No wonder the Ojibwa thought the gnarled cedar a holy tree.
For centuries it stood on its barren rock
high above Lake Superior.
Fierce winds twisted its trunk in a spiral
from top to bottom, stripped away its bark.
Holes gaped where branches had been torn away.
Winter snow and ice storms had failed to kill the tree.
A few short branches at the top still had bark and leaves.

In time, after an exceedingly mild winter,
the ancient tree produced a seed.
And from that seed,
through the relentless perseverance of nature,
had grown a new young cedar, straight and tall.

A Basket of Stones

A small basket of stones rests on my low bookcase.
They are all the same color, a soft blue gray,
Most are round, some few are oval—
an ideal shape for skipping.
They have been tumbled, smoothed, by the waters of
    Lake Superior
the largest, coldest, deepest, most northern of the
    Great Lakes.

The beach at Grand Marais was filled with them, no sand.
We gathered them that day as if they were precious jewels,
another and another and another. Why? Why did we want
more and more when they were so much the same?

Did we feel some vestige of the elemental power
of the waves that had smoothed them?
The relentless energy over years, centuries, eons?
Did we sense the mystery of the vast force that had
    shaped them?

They are not beautiful like the amethyst, the rose quartz,
    the crystal, the malachite
that I have gathered, but if I had to choose just one
    collection to keep
I would choose my basket of blue gray stones.

Gulls

"Birds," I said, "wooden birds" —
for the long blank wall
in the upper hallway
of my new town house.

Wooden birds were not flying that year,
only metal —
cold, hard-edged metal.

Someone told me of the Norwegian woodcarver
west of the Twin Cities
some miles beyond Wayzata,
a gnome of a man
with the bluest eyes I have ever seen.
(They hadn't mentioned the eyes.)

Yes, yes, he understood.
He would call when they were done.

I drove west again, eagerly, apprehensively.
He brought them out into the garden,
laid them on a table,
then watched, almost holding his breath,
as I looked.

They were gorgeous, two gulls in flight,
the feathers carefully delineated

in the outspread wings,
the larger one leading the smaller,
up, up into the heavens.

"If I could carve," I said, "this is what I would have made."

His face broke into a smile.
His blue eyes shone even more intensely blue.
He had gone to the North Shore of Lake Superior.
He had taken forty — forty! — rolls of film
of the ubiquitous gulls.
The wood was a mellow butternut.
Clearly he had loved what he was doing.

The gulls flew for years in my upstairs hall,
untrammeled, heading toward the sun.
They fly now in a very different setting
above my desk, soaring into the heavens,
free spirits always.

Made in the USA
Charleston, SC
30 March 2011